MW01291831

Squids Will Be Squids

What Are Squids?

By Lisa Strattin

© 2013 Lisa Strattin

Revised © 2019

FREE EBOOK!

http://LisaStrattin.com/Subscribe-Here

BOX SET

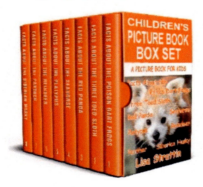

LisaStrattin.com/BookBundle

Facts for Kids Picture Books by Lisa Strattin

Sign Up for New Release Emails Here

http://lisastrattin.com/subscribe-here

All rights reserved. No part of this book may be reproduced by any means whatsoever without the written permission from the author, except brief portions quoted for purpose of review.

All information in this book has been carefully researched and checked for factual accuracy. However, the author and publisher makes no warranty, express or implied, that the information contained herein is appropriate for every individual, situation or purpose and assume no responsibility for errors or omissions. The reader assumes the risk and full responsibility for all actions, and the author will not be held responsible for any loss or damage, whether consequential, incidental, special or otherwise, that may result from the information presented in this book.

All images are purchased from stock photo sites or royalty free for commercial use.

I have relied on my own observations as well as many different sources for this book and I have done my best to check facts and give credit where it is due. In the event that any material is used without proper permission, please contact me so that the oversight can be corrected.

Contents

WHAT ARE SQUIDS?

The ocean is full of amazing marine life, but there is nothing as cool as the squid. Squids can be large, small, and sometimes they can even be scary! What are squids exactly? What do they eat? How do they survive? Can they live outside of water? Will you see them roaming around your neighborhood anytime soon?

The first thing you need to know, is that there are about 300 different squid species, all of which feature a distinct head, a mantle, and of course, eight arms.

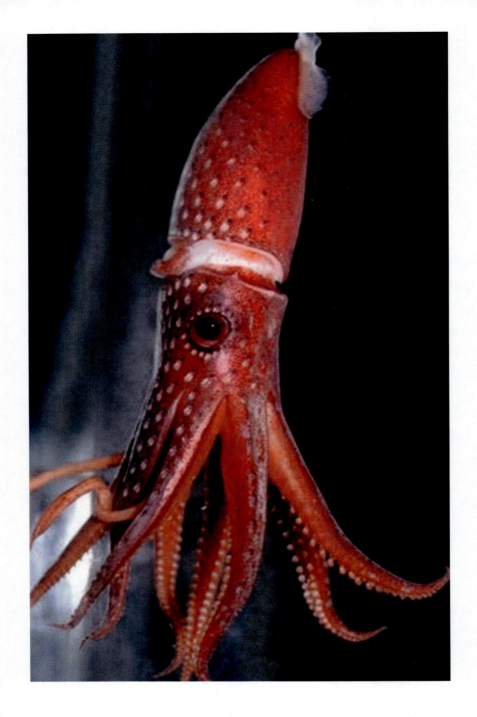

What many people don't know is that some squid species can actually fly over the surface of the water for short distances! They won't take flight like a bird, but on the high seas you might just see one here and there!

The main body of the squid is called the mantle, and on each side is a large swimming fin. Unlike many species in the ocean, the squid can become invisible! All over the skin you will find special cells containing pigment which allow the squid to change to virtually any color -- matching its surroundings perfectly.

Wouldn't it be fun to be able to change colors any time you wanted?

COLOR ME

SQUID STAGES OF GROWTH

Baby squids are larvae when they hatch, and most don't live very long once they reach squid adulthood. It is commonly believed that short finned squids do not live much longer than 12-18 months.

Squids are normally a species that lay eggs in groups, and the females release nearly 11 pounds of eggs during their cycle. There are some that carry their eggs in their arms to keep them from danger. Unfortunately, adult squids die shortly after they find a mate and lay their eggs.

Even though there are many different creatures in the ocean, the squid is one of the most fascinating.

COLOR ME

FIVE TYPES OF SQUIDS

Giant Squid: As the name sounds, the giant squid is huge. In fact, the average length of a female is about 43 feet! Despite their large size, however, they are anatomically the same as any other squid.

COLOR ME

Colossal Squid: While this squid is mostly like all the other squids, it has eyes larger than any other creature on earth. It can watch you and the rest of the ocean at the same time! It is much larger than the giant squid, and is thought to be the very largest one. It weighs a whopping 1,000 pounds and can grow up to 46 feet long.

18

COLOR ME

Humboldt Squid: Though they are often called a "Jumbo Squid," they are only about 7 feet long and 100 pounds. They're still big, but they're nowhere near as big as the colossal and giant squids.

Japanese Flying Squid: Remember when we mentioned that some squids can fly? Well, here they are! Not many people know about the Japanese Flying Squid, but they have distinct features that make them unique from others in the ocean.

COLOR ME

Vampire Squid: This isn't a sparkly squid, nor one that will suck your blood in a dark alley at night, but it is a very dark, color and it does feature long arms that flow like a black cape. For this reason, the vampire squid reminds more than a few people of Dracula.

COLOR ME

WHAT DO SQUIDS EAT?

All squids are different, but they usually eat other marine life. They are meat eaters, and with that being the case, depending on the size of the squid, a whale might actually be on the menu. The squid is capable of eating anything that its tentacles are able to latch onto. This makes the squid one of the most aggressive and dangerous animals in the underwater kingdom.

COLOR ME

HOW LONG DO SQUIDS LIVE?

Squids do not live very long. In fact, they only live two to three years, although the giant squid can live for three to five years. When they reach one year of age, they are considered mature, and the females die shortly after laying their eggs. It's amazing to think that these creatures grow so large in such a short time.

COLOR ME

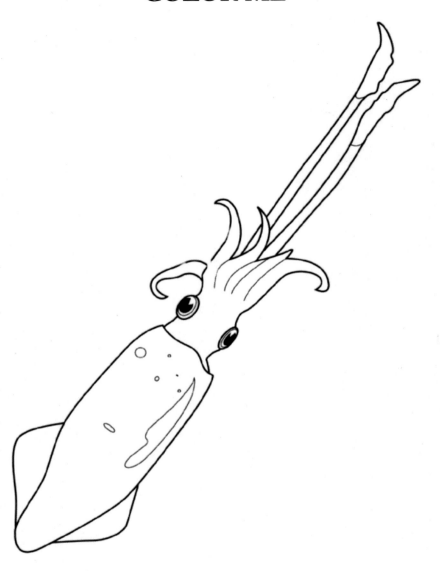

ARE SQUIDS DANGEROUS?

When we ask if squids are dangerous, we really want to know if they are dangerous to human beings. The answer is a resounding yes. While they might not be a creature we see often, they will attack anything they can latch onto. In addition, they can spray any enemies with black ink before shredding them with their tentacles.

Underwater, with their offensive abilities and their camouflage, they have the advantage. You remember they can change colors, right?

Squids are amazing, yet extremely dangerous. They roam the oceans, preying on the weak and strong alike. You'd be lucky to see one, but don't get in their way!

COLOR ME

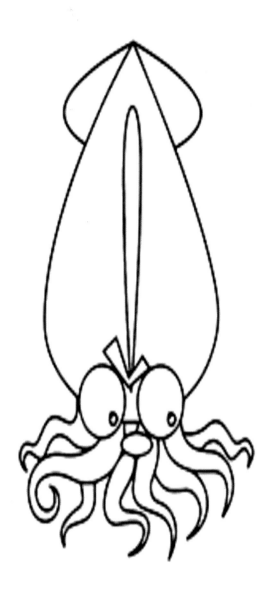

Please leave me a review here:

http://lisastrattin.com/reviewsquids

For more Kindle Downloads Visit Lisa Strattin Author Page on Amazon Author Central

http://amazon.com/author/lisastrattin

To see upcoming titles, visit my website at LisaStrattin.com– all books available on kindle!

http://lisastrattin.com

FREE EBOOK!

http://LisaStrattin.com/Subscribe-Here

LisaStrattin.com/Facebook

LisaStrattin.com/Youtube

LisaStrattin.com/BookBundle

Made in the USA
Coppell, TX
02 November 2022

85641321R00026